Gluten-Free Desserts Cookbook

Your Go-To Gluten Free Book

Thomas Kelley

INTRODUCTION

What is gluten? This question may pop up in one's mind as today many people are going gluten-free. Gluten is one of the most complex forms of protein that contains large molecules which our stomach finds difficult to digest. Wheat flour, barley and rye are common examples of gluten filled elements.

Baking involves major gluten filled ingredients like flour and yeast, making it harder for someone with a sweet tooth to avoid gluten altogether. Desserts that you eat from the store or at restaurants are mostly all heavily packed with gluten therefore the only resort you have is to make your own gluten-free desserts at home which are equally delicious.

Baking may seem like a challenging task at first mainly due to the beautifully decorated desserts that we are served in the restaurants. One may assume that this masterpiece can only be created by expert chefs and there is no way that it can be done at home.

This gluten-free cookbook will put an end to all such misconceptions. We have compiled 30 delectable dessert recipes with no traces of gluten. Each recipe has its unique indulging taste. You don't have to be an expert to make these recipes, but instead you must have the love to eat indulging desserts and you should enjoy baking.

This Gluten-free dessert cookbook includes recipes like chocolate pots, rice pudding, chocolate cake, chocolate-dipped espresso meringues, maple baked apples and the list goes on. These recipes have been simplified for you so that you not only enjoy eating them but also enjoy making them and executing your own masterpiece and dazzle everyone.

TABLE OF CONTENTS

CHOCOLATE POTS

The word chocolate lights up everybody's eyes. Who doesn't enjoy a delicious yet simple dessert made entirely with chocolate? Every bite of these chocolate pots is filled with the deliciousness of chocolate.

Servings:	8
Preparation Time:	30 minutes

INGREDIENTS:

- Bittersweet chocolate, 6 oz. chopped
- Granulated sugar, 2/3 cup
- Whole milk, 3 cups
- Egg yolks, 4
- Unsweetened cocoa powder, ½ teaspoon
- Cornstarch, 2 tablespoons
- Pure vanilla extract, ½ teaspoon
- Kosher salt, 1/8 teaspoon

METHOD:

1. Add together cornstarch, salt and sugar. Pour 1/3 cup whole milk and combine well making a paste.
2. Beat egg yolks and stir in the paste. Add remaining whole milk and stir gently to combine well.
3. Cook this mixture on medium-low flame for 15 minutes while stirring continuously. You don't want to boil the mixture instead just mix until it thickens.
4. Add chocolate and mix.
5. Add vanilla extract and keep stirring to melt the chocolate. When you have achieved a smooth consistency, transfer the mixture into ramekins and cover.
6. Refrigerate overnight or for 2 hours at least.
   Dust cocoa powder and serve.

RASPBERRY ICE

Looking for a simple treat to serve after dinner tonight? Try out this easy raspberry ice recipe and enjoy the sweetness. All you have to do is simply puree some frozen or fresh raspberries and blend them with fine syrup and refrigerate. Serve chilled.

Servings: 4

Preparation Time: 10 minutes

INGREDIENTS:

- Raspberries, 3 cups
- Heavy cream, ½ cup
- Sugar, ½ cup
- Water, 1 cup

METHOD:

1. Mix sugar and water together and cook on medium flame while stirring frequently. When boiled, keep aside to cool.
2. Puree raspberries with syrup in a food processor and strain in the serving bowl.
3. Refrigerate for 5 hours.
4. Whip cream until fluffy and soft peaks are formed.
5. Scoop cream on top and serve.

Buttermilk Pudding

This is a delicate pudding recipe made with buttermilk, unflavored gelatin, vanilla and folded in heavy cream. This recipe will require only 15 minutes of your time and will serve 5 to 6 people conveniently.

Servings: 6

Preparation Time: 15 minutes

INGREDIENTS:

- Buttermilk, 2 cups
- Unflavored gelatin, 1 ¼ oz. envelope
- Vanilla extract, 1 teaspoon
- Heavy cream, 1 cup
- Sugar, 2/3 cup

METHOD:

1. Mix gelation with ¼ cup water and keep aside for 3 minutes.
2. Cook ½ cup heavy cream with sugar on low flame. When the sugar dissolves completely, remove from flame and add gelatin.
3. Combine remaining heavy cream with vanilla, gelatin-cream mixture and buttermilk. Fold everything well.
4. Grease ramekins and ladle the mixture in each ramekin and cover.
5. Refrigerate for at least 3 hours or overnight.
6. Top it with blueberries or raspberries if you like. Serve chilled.

MAPLE BAKED APPLES

Maple baked apples are coated in succulent maple sauce and sated with a combination of raisins and walnuts. Bake these fine apples until they are tender and leave their juices to blend with other ingredients for a divine taste.

Servings: 4

Preparation Time: 20 minutes

INGREDIENTS:

- Apple, 4 large
- Golden raisins, ¼ cup
- Maple syrup, ¾ cup
- Ice cream, for serving
- Walnut pieces, ½ cup
- Unsalted butter pieces, 2 tablespoons

METHOD:

1. Preheat the oven to 400 F.
2. Core and trim the apples from bottom and lay them flat on a baking dish.
3. Pour maple syrup on apples and stuff with walnuts and raisins.
4. Place each butter piece on top of each apple and bake for 50 minutes.
5. When the apples are ready transfer the liquid on the baking dish in a pan and bring to a boil. Decrease the flame and cook until it forms a thick sauce.
6. Ladle the sauce over apples and serve with ice cream on aside.

COCONUT RICE CUSTARD

This custard is made from white rice simmered in coconut milk. These custard bowls are so light yet fulfilling at the same time. You can garnish rice pudding with chopped pistachio or almonds.

Servings: 6

Preparation Time: 1 hour 20 minutes

INGREDIENTS:

- Long-grain white rice, 1 cup
- Unsweetened coconut milk, 1 can
- Vanilla extract, 1 teaspoon
- Water, ¼ cup
- Half-and-half, 3 cups
- Sugar, ¼ + 2/3 cup
- Eggs, 5

METHOD:

1. Preheat the oven to 325 F.
2. Boil coconut milk with ¼ cup sugar and water.
3. Add rice and simmer on low flame for 20 minutes or until rice gets tender. Cover the lid.
4. Cook half-and-half on low flame.
5. Beat eggs with remaining sugar and vanilla until fluffy,
6. Ladle half-and-half gradually in the egg mixture and combine well.
7. Add rice and mix.
8. Pour the mixture in a baking dish. Place the baking dish in a water filled roasting pan and bake for 1 hour or until set.
9. Serve.

RASPBERRY SORBET WITH WHIPPED CREAM AND MERINGUES

Top the sorbet with delicious meringues that will simply melt in your mouth in every bite. If you want you can add a few drops of food color in your cream for extra color.

Image Credit: Flickr user Istelleinad,
<https://www.flickr.com/photos/istelleinad/3993484309/sizes/o/>

Servings: 8

Preparation Time: 10 minutes

INGREDIENTS:

- Raspberry sorbet, 2 pints
- Heavy cream, 1 cup
- Meringue cookies, 16 small
- Confectioners' sugar, 2 tablespoons

METHOD:

1. Whip cream with sugar and form soft peaks.
2. Break cookies into small pieces in a bowl.
3. Put sorbet in each serving bowl and top it with cream and cookies.

POACHED PEARS

Ripe pears when poached in red wine take on a vivid burgundy shade. Cloves give these pears a strong hint of flavor whereas the cinnamon stick adds a bittersweet taste to it. Serve them with whipped cream on the side.

Servings: 4

Preparation Time: 55 minutes

INGREDIENTS:

- Ripe pears, 4 small and peeled
- Red wine, 1 ½ cups
- Cloves, 5
- Navel orange, 1, quartered
- Cinnamon stick, 1
- Lemon, 1
- Sugar, ¾ cup
- Vanilla extract, ¼ teaspoon

METHOD:

1. Mix red wine with orange and lemon juice. Add cloves, sugar, cinnamon stick and vanilla.
2. Coat pears in the mixture and bring to a boil.
3. Decrease the flame and let it simmer for 25 minutes.
4. When pears are tender transfer them to the serving plate.
5. Strain the mixture in a bowl. Put the mixture back in the saucepan and simmer for 15 minutes.
6. Drizzle the syrup over pears and serve.

CHOCOLATE CAKE

This chocolate cake has no traces of flour yet is more delicious than any you buy from the bakery. The texture of this cake is dense and rich. Serve each cake slice with whipped cream on the side.

Servings: 10

Preparation Time: 120 minutes

INGREDIENTS:

- Bittersweet chocolate, 8 oz. chopped
- Sour cream/crème fraiche, ½ cup
- Heavy cream, 1 ¼ cup
- Confectioners' sugar, ¼ cup
- Unsalted butter, 1 cup, cubes
- Eggs, 5 large
- Granulated sugar, 1 cup
- Unsweetened cocoa powder, ¼ cup

METHOD:

1. Preheat the oven to 350 F.
2. Grease a 9 inch pan with butter and dust with a dash of cocoa powder.
3. Melt butter in a saucepan and add ¼ cup heavy cream. Cook over medium flame.
4. Now add chocolate and melt. Stir constantly. When melted and forms a smooth mixture remove from flame and keep aside.
5. Beat eggs with granulated sugar and cocoa powder until fluffy.
6. Add melted chocolate and fold in together.
7. Add this mixture in the greased pan and bake for around 35 minutes or until puffed.
8. Leave the cake in the pan to cool down for 1 hour.
9. Beat 1 cup heavy cream with crème fraiche and confectioners' sugar.
10. Serve the cake with whipped cream.

RASPBERRY FOOL

Mashed raspberries folded in heavy cream will wonderfully melt in your mouth. This is one of the easiest recipes to try. The great part about this is that you can replace or add different berries or fruit in the same recipe.

Servings: 4-6

Preparation Time: 10 minutes

INGREDIENTS:

- Raspberries, 2 cups
- Heavy cream, 1 ½ cups
- Sugar, ½ cup

METHOD:

1. Mash raspberries a little and add ¼ cup sugar. Mix well.
2. Combine sugar and cream together and whip until stiff.
3. Now combine raspberries and cream together. Refrigerate to chill.
4. Scoop into serving bowls and enjoy.

Vanilla Pudding with sautéed Pears

The ripe pears sautéed in unsalted butter and sugar give a slight crunchy and sweet flavor. Top the pears in a delightful and delectable homemade vanilla pudding and dust a dash of cinnamon for enhanced flavor.

Servings: 4

Preparation Time: 20 minutes

INGREDIENTS:

For the pudding:
- Cornstarch, ¼ cup
- Whole milk, 2 ½ cups
- Vanilla, 1 ½ teaspoons
- Salt, ¼ teaspoon
- Sugar, 1/3 cup
- Unsalted butter, 2 tablespoons. Melted
- Eggs, 4
- Unsalted butter, 2 tablespoons, not melted

For sautéed pears:
- Pears, 2
- Ground cinnamon
- Unsalted butter, 2 tablespoons
- Sugar, 2 tablespoons

METHOD:

1. Mix cornstarch with 1/3 cup sugar, eggs and salt. Add milk gradually and whisk until combined.
2. Simmer pudding on low flame while stirring consistently for 3 minutes.
3. Remove the saucepan from flame and add melted butter and vanilla.
4. Transfer the mixture in a bowl and line the surface with waxed paper.
5. Refrigerate for 1 hour.
6. Meanwhile core the ends of the pears and slice thinly.
7. Melt butter and sauté pears for 3 minutes.
8. Sprinkle sugar and combine for 3 minutes or until golden.
9. Transfer the chilled pudding into serving cups place pears on top.
10. Dust ground cinnamon and serve.

CHOCOLATE-DIPPED ESPRESSO MERINGUES

A bitter-sweet combination of chocolate and coffee is what makes these cookies one of a kind. They are prepared with espresso powder, cream of tartar, vanilla and eggs and then dipped into melted chocolate. These can be stored in an airtight jar for 3 days.

Image Credit: Flickr user Veganbaking.net, <https://www.flickr.com/photos/vegan-baking/5457765026/>

Servings: 24 meringues

Preparation Time: 30 minutes

INGREDIENTS:

- Instant espresso powder, 1 teaspoon
- Cream of tartar, 1 pinch
- Egg whites, 2 large
- Sugar, 1 cup
- Vanilla extract, 1 teaspoon
- Kosher salt, ¼ teaspoon
- Bittersweet chocolate, 4 oz. melted and cooled

METHOD:

1. Preheat the oven to 200 F.
2. Combine egg whites with cream of tartar, vanilla, salt and espresso powder. Beat until soft peaks are formed. Add sugar 1 tablespoon at a time and beat on high speed until glossy.
3. Line a baking sheet with parchment paper and place scoops of the mixture on it.
4. Bake for 2 hours. Meringues need to be firm and dry.
5. Let the meringues cool down in the oven for 1 hour with the oven door slightly open.
6. When the meringues are completely cool, dip each meringue in melted chocolate and place it back on the parchment paper.
7. Refrigerate for 30 minutes.
8. Serve when chocolate is set.

Marshmallow Cookies with Mini Chips

These cookies are super chewy and gooey and leave a sweet aftertaste. Make sure you use gluten-free cookie mix and chocolate mini chips. These cookies can be stored in an airtight jar for up to 3 days.

Servings: 54 cookies

Preparation Time: 20 minutes

INGREDIENTS:

- Semisweet chocolate mini chips, ¼ cup (should be gluten-free)
- Ground cinnamon, 1 teaspoon
- Sweetened dried cranberries, ¼ cup
- Water, 2 tablespoons
- Ground nutmeg, 1/8 teaspoon
- Toasted pecans, ¼ cup, coarsely chopped
- Cookie mix, 1 package (should be gluten-free)
- Miniature marshmallows, 2/3 cup
- Eggs, 2 large
- Canola oil, ½ cup

METHOD:

1. Preheat the oven to 350 F.
2. Blend eggs with water and canola oil on medium speed until well combined.
3. Add cookie mix, nutmeg and cinnamon and beat again.
4. Add pecans, marshmallows, cranberries and mini chips. Fold in well.
5. Drop heaping tablespoons of the mixture on a parchment lined baking sheet and bake for 15 minutes.
6. Cool at room temperature and serve.

STRAWBERRY GRANITA

This Granita contains chilled strawberry scrape topped with lemon zest and strawberry chunks for a sweet and citrusy hint of flavors. This recipe is a great way to spruce up a hot summer afternoon.

Servings: 4
Preparation Time: 5 minutes
Freezing Time: 5 hours

INGREDIENTS:

- Strawberries, 3 cups, sliced
- Sugar, ½ cup
- Lemon juice, 2 tablespoons
- Warm water, ½ cup

METHOD:

1. Blend sugar and water in a blender and dissolve the sugar.
2. Now stir lemon juice and strawberries and blend again to make a smooth mixture.
3. Ladle the processed mixture in squared baking dish and cover.
4. Freeze for 3 hours.
5. Stir the frozen mixture and cover the dish and freeze for additional 5 hours.
6. When set keep the mixture for 10 minutes at room temperature.
7. Use a fork to scrape the mixture and serve.

VANILLA-CHOCOLATE PUDDING POPS

For this recipe you can simply follow the vanilla pudding recipe at number 10 and turn it into delicious popsicles coated with chocolate. For the sake of creativity you can drizzle strawberry sauce or toasted pecans on top.

Image Credit: Flickr user Jennifer Chalt,
<https://www.flickr.com/photos/9174828@N04/13828899745/>

Servings: 4

Preparation Time: 5 minutes

Freezing Time: 3 hours

INGREDIENTS:

- Bittersweet chocolate, 2 oz. melted
- Vanilla pudding, 2 cups

METHOD:

1. Place the warm pudding into two bowls and add melted chocolate in one bowl and mix.
2. Cover the bowls with plastic and refrigerate for 30 minutes.
3. Ladle ¼ cup of chocolate pudding in ice-pop molds keep for 10 minutes in the freezer.
4. Ladle another ¼ cup of vanilla pudding in each mold.
5. Place wooden sticks in each pudding mold and freeze again for 3 hours.

Nectarines Poached in Lavender-Honey Syrup

This is a very unique recipe of nectarines and lavender. Lavender syrup is sweet and filled with herbal properties. Nectarine when poached in lavender syrup becomes tender and leaves its juices that blend perfectly with other ingredients.

Servings: 12
Preparation Time: 20 minutes

INGREDIENTS:

- Nectarines, 6, halved and pitted
- Honey, ¾ cup
- Water, 4 cups
- Dried lavender buds, 2 teaspoons
- Sugar, ¾ cup
- Fresh lavender sprigs
- Vanilla low-fat frozen yogurt, 6 cups

METHOD:

1. Combine honey, sugar and water in a saucepan and bring to a boil to dissolve.
2. Add lavender bugs and nectarines.
3. Decrease the flame and simmer for 8 minutes.
4. Use a slotted spoon to remove nectarines from the liquid.
5. Once again boil the liquid for 10 minutes.
6. Place the nectarines on serving plates with yoghurt and ladle the syrup on top. Decorate with lavender sprigs.

CHOCOLATE ESPRESSO MOUSSE

This recipe makes a bitter-sweet chocolate mousse that will delightfully melt in your mouth. Mousse is great because it requires little preparation time and can be made a day ahead and refrigerated.

Servings: 8

Preparation Time: 20 minutes

INGREDIENTS:

- Semisweet chocolate, 8 oz. chopped
- Instant espresso powder, 2 teaspoons
- Heavy cream, 2 cups
- Egg yolks, 3 large
- Granulated sugar, 6 tablespoons

METHOD:

1. Melt chocolate and set aside to cool.
2. Combine espresso powder with ¾ cup of heavy cream, egg yolks and 4 tablespoon of sugar and cook on medium flame for 3 minutes.
3. Strain the mixture in the bowl of melted chocolate and fold until smooth and glossy.
4. Refrigerate for 30 minutes.
5. Beat the remaining heavy cream with sugar until peaks are stiff.
6. Fold whipped cream in 3 intervals in the chocolate mixture.
7. Refrigerate for 30 minutes.
8. Top with chopped chocolate before serving.

CARROT CAKE

Each bite of this delicious carrot cake is so moist. Make sure you use gluten-free pudding and yellow cake mix. For a colorful effect you can add a few drops of food color of your choice in the frosting.

Servings: 22

Preparation Time: 20 minutes

INGREDIENTS:

- Yellow cake mix, 1 package
- Grated orange rind, 1 teaspoon
- Walnuts, ¾ cup, chopped
- Vegetable oil, ½ cup
- Vanilla instant pudding mix, 1 package
- Fresh Orange juice, 2/3 cup
- Ground cinnamon, 2 teaspoons
- Carrots, 3 1/3 cups, grated
- Eggs, 4 large
- Raisins, ¾ cup

For frosting:
- 1% low-fat milk, 2 tablespoons
- Powdered sugar, 4 ½ cups, sifted
- Vanilla extract, 1 ½ teaspoons
- 1/3 less fat cream cheese, 6 oz. softened

METHOD:

1. Preheat the oven to 350 F.
2. Combine cake mix with ground cinnamon, pudding mix, orange juice and rind, eggs and vegetable oil. Beat on low speed for a minute then medium-high for 5 minutes.
3. Add carrots and fold in gently. Add raisins and walnuts and fold again.
4. Grease pan with cooking spray and pour the batter evenly.
5. Bake for 30 minutes.
6. Let the cake cool.
7. Combine cream cheese with vanilla and milk and beat on high speed.
8. Add sugar in intervals and beat on low until smooth.
9. Slice the cake horizontally in halve.

10. Place one layer on the cake dish and coat it with ½ cup frosting. Place other cake layer and coat with the remaining frosting.
11. Serve.

Mango and Coconut Ring

A seasonal summer dessert made with mango puree, heavy cream and coconut cream, the mango and coconut ring is a delight. The colorful yellow top looks elegant and it's hard to believe that this classy dessert is so easy to make.

Servings: 6

Preparation Time: 25 minutes

INGREDIENTS:

- Mangoes, 2, ripe, peeled and pitted
- Lime juice, 1 teaspoon
- Egg whites, 3 large
- Canola oil
- Heavy cream, 1 cup
- Sugar, 1/3 cup
- Coconut cream, ½ cup

METHOD:

1. Puree mangoes with lime juice in a blender until smooth.
2. Grease a gelation mold and transfer the puree in it. Keep aside.
3. Beat heavy cream with coconut cream and refrigerate.
4. Combine egg whites with sugar and beat until stiff.
5. Fold egg mixture with whipped cream and transfer to the gelatin mold. Spread evenly and refrigerate overnight.
6. Serve chilled.

ALMOND CRÈME CARAMEL

This decadent dessert looks so divine and tastes so delectable that it leaves the impression that you spent several hours in the kitchen. The secret behind this deliciousness is just 8 ingredients and dedication.

Servings: 9

Preparation Time: 25 minutes

INGREDIENTS:

- Fat-free sweetened condensed milk, 1 can
- Sugar, ½ cup
- Toasted almonds, sliced
- Almond extract, ½ teaspoon
- Eggs, 4 large
- Almonds, ¼ cup, coarsely chopped
- Vanilla extract, 1 teaspoon
- Evaporated fat-free milk, 1 can

METHOD:

1. Preheat the oven to 350 F.
2. Coat the surface of a pan with sugar and place on medium heat for 6 minutes.
3. When the sugar turns golden remove and keep aside.
4. Beat eggs until foamy. Add vanilla, ¼ cup almonds and both milks. Combine well and transfer to the pan coated with sugar.
5. Fill a large baking dish with water and place the other pan in it.
6. Bake for 55 minutes.
7. When the cake cools down transfer to the serving plate and garnish with sliced almonds.
8. Serve.

SLICED ORANGES AND PEARS WITH MINT SUGAR

This is a quick recipe when you are craving something sweet or have guests coming over. You can add berries of your choice and serve with whipped cream or ice cream.

Servings: 4

Preparation Time: 10 minutes

INGREDIENTS:

- Pears, 2, cored and sliced into wedges
- Oranges, 2, peeled and sliced
- Sugar, 2 tablespoons
- Mint leaves, 2 tablespoons

METHOD:

1. Place the fruits mix in serving bowls.
2. Chop mint leaves very finely.
3. Mix sugar and mint leaves together and sprinkle over the fruits.
4. Enjoy.

Piña Colada Cheesecake Bars

Coconut flour is healthy and also gluten-free. For graham cracker crumbs make sure you are using a gluten-free package. Coconut flour is sweet so level the quantity of sugar according to your preference.

Servings: 16

Preparation Time: 30 minutes

INGREDIENTS:

- Graham cracker crumbs, 1 cup
- Turbinado sugar, 2 tablespoons
- 2% low fat cottage cheese, 1 cup
- Coconut flour, 2 tablespoons
- Vanilla extract, ½ teaspoon
- Water, 1 tablespoon
- Fresh pineapples, 1 cup, chopped
- Canola oil, 1 tablespoon
- Ground ginger, ½ teaspoon
- Fresh lemon juice, 1 tablespoon
- Grated lemon rind, 1 ½ tablespoons
- Egg, ¾ cup
- Unsweetened coconut, ¼ cup, shredded and toasted
- Salt
- Pineapple juice, 1 tablespoon
- Block style fat free cream cheese, ¼ cup
- Butter, 2 tablespoons, melted
- Sugar, ½ cup

METHOD:

1. Preheat the oven to 350 F.
2. Combine Graham crackers with coconut flour, ground ginger and turbinado sugar. Add water, oil and butter. Mix well and transfer to a square baking pan.
3. Bake for 10 minutes.
4. Let it cool.
5. Combine cottage cheese with sugar, pineapple juice, eggs, pineapples, lemon juice, lemon rind, salt and vanilla.
6. Process in a blender until smooth.
7. Transfer the mixture to the pan and spread over the crust evenly.

8. Bake for 30 minutes.
9. Let it cool for 10 minutes on room temperature before refrigerating.
10. Refrigerate for 2 hours.
11. Garnish with shredded coconut and pineapple chunks.
12. Slice them into 16 small bars

ARCTIC LIME FREEZE

Homemade ice cream is simply delicious and super easy to make. If you have an ice cream freezer at home then freeze the mixture according to the directions of your appliance. For those of you who don't have one, you can simply freeze the mixture in a plastic can.

Servings:	5
Preparation Time:	10 minutes
Freezing Time:	2 hours

INGREDIENTS:

- Low-fat silken firm tofu, 1 package, drained
- Grated lime rind
- Limeade concentrate, 1 can, thawed and undiluted
- Mint sprigs
- Water, 1 ½ cups

METHOD:

1. Process limeade and tofu in a food processor until smooth.
2. Stir water and process a little to incorporate.
3. Ladle the mixture in an ice cream can and cover.
4. Refrigerate for 2 hours.
5. Serve with rind and mint atop.

MOROCCAN-SPICED ORANGES

This juicy treat can be ready within minutes. Make sure you toss the oranges well with the contents. Serve with ice cream or frozen yogurt. If you don't like the flavor of cinnamon don't sprinkle it while serving.

Servings: 4

Preparation Time: 10 minutes

INGREDIENTS:

- Orange sections, 2 ½ cups, cut into ½ inch pieces
- Ground cinnamon
- Silvered almonds, ¼ cup
- Fresh lemon juice, 1 tablespoon
- Grated orange rind
- Dates, 4, chopped and pitted
- Ground cinnamon, ¼ teaspoon
- Powdered sugar, 1 tablespoon

METHOD:

1. Mix oranges with almonds, dates and lemon juice.
2. Dust with sugar and cinnamon.
3. Toss well to incorporate.
4. Cover and refrigerate for 20-25 minutes.
5. Sprinkle some rind and more cinnamon before serving.

BITTERSWEET CHOCOLATE SORBET

If you take a glimpse at the ingredients you will not agree that this sorbet is actually low-fat. Each scoop of chocolate sorbet is rich and indulging and making you crave for more. Yet it's also relatively low on calories so you can enjoy it guilt-free.

Servings:	4
Preparation Time:	10 minutes
Freezing Time:	2 hours

INGREDIENTS:

- bittersweet chocolate, 3 oz. chopped
- Sugar, 1 ¼ cups
- Vanilla, 2 teaspoon
- Unsweetened Cocoa, ½ cup
- Water, 2/2 cups

METHOD:

1. Boil water and add cocoa and sugar.
2. Reduce the flame and simmer for 5 minutes while stirring constantly.
3. Remove from flame and stir vanilla and chocolate.
4. Mix well to melt the chocolate completely. Cover and leave for 10 minutes on room temperature.
5. Ladle the mixture into a freezer can and cover.
6. Refrigerate for 2 hours.

Mocha Cream Brownie with Fresh Raspberries

Who would believe that a small box of brownie mix can execute such divine and heavenly brownies? In addition to raspberries you can also use blackberries, cherry and strawberries.

Servings: 12

Preparation Time: 60 minutes

INGREDIENTS:

- Brownie mix, 1 package
- Instant coffee granules, 2 teaspoons
- Canola oil, 6 tablespoons
- Raspberries, 1 ½ cups
- Egg whites, 4 large
- Vanilla extract, ½ teaspoon
- Instant coffee granules, 1 tablespoon
- Chocolate syrup, ½ cup
- Heavy whipping cream, 1 cup
- Powdered sugar, ¼ cup

METHOD:

1. Preheat the oven to 350 F.
2. Beat eggs until frothy and pour in the brownie mix.
3. Add oil and 1 tablespoon coffee. Combine well.
4. Pour the batter in a greased baking dish of 11 x 7 inch.
5. Bake for 22 minutes. When the brownies cools completely, slice into 12 triangles.
6. Now combine whipped cream with remaining coffee and vanilla. Whip on high speed and form a foamy mixture.
7. Add sugar and whip again.
8. Either place brownies on serving plates individually or on 1 large serving dish. Drizzle chocolate syrup and scoops on whipped cream on each brownie. Top it with raspberries and enjoy.

PEANUT-BUTTER COOKIES

Completely flourless cookies made with peanut butter, brown sugar, vanilla, sugar and eggs, there are keepers. These cookies have a chewy and nutty texture and can be stored up to a week in an airtight jar.

Servings: 36 cookies

Preparation Time: 30 minutes

INGREDIENTS:

- Creamy peanut butter, 2 cups
- Packed Light brown sugar, ½ cup
- Kosher salt, ½ teaspoon
- Granulated sugar, 1 ½ cups
- Baking soda, 2 teaspoons
- Eggs, 2 large
- Vanilla, 2 teaspoon

METHOD:

1. Preheat the oven to 350 F.
2. Beat peanut butter and sugar together on high speed for 3 minutes.
3. Add eggs, salt, baking soda and vanilla. Beat on low until well combined.
4. Take spoonful of the mixture and place on a prepared baking sheet.
5. Dust some flour on a fork and press each cookie slightly and make a crisscross outline.
6. Bake for 12 minutes rotating the cookie sheet in between.
7. Let the cookies cool on wire rack.
8. Enjoy.

PEACH AND RASPBERRY PARFAIT

Peaches and raspberries when combined with lemon juice and sugar, leave their own juices which makes citrusy and saccharine syrup. This recipe is a great way to complement any ice cream.

Servings: 4

Preparation Time: 25 minutes

INGREDIENTS:

- Peaches, 2, sliced into 2 ½ pieces
- Sugar, 2 tablespoons
- Lemon juice, 1 tablespoon
- Raspberries, 1 ½ cups
- Vanilla ice cream, 1 pint

METHOD:

1. Toss peach and raspberries in lemon juice and sugar. Let it stand for 20 minutes.
2. Scoop ice cream into individual serving bowls and top it with fruits and its syrup.
3. Enjoy.

Pumpkin Cheesecake Bites

Pumpkin season is just around the corner and this recipe is a great way to enjoy this healthy and delicious food. This recipe requires no baking, just a little freezing time which is not much considering the ease it provides.

Servings: 16 squares

Preparation Time: 20 minutes

INGREDIENTS:

For crust:
- Dates, 1 cup, pitted
- Almond milk, 1 tablespoon
- Cacao powder, 1 tablespoon
- Almond flour, ½ cup
- Vanilla, 2 teaspoon

Cheesecake layers:
- Raw cashews, 1 ½ cups
- Pumpkin spice, 1 teaspoon
- Maple syrup, 1/3 cup
- Pumpkin, 1/3 cup, canned

METHOD:

1. Soak nuts in water for an hour. Drain and keep aside.
2. Process the crust ingredients in a food processor for 1 minute.
3. Spread the mixture on a parchment lined loaf pan and refrigerate to set.
4. Meanwhile prepare topping.
5. Process all cheesecake ingredients in the food processor until smooth.
6. Take out the loaf pan from the freezer and spread the cake mixture over the crust. Refrigerate again for 2 hours.
7. When the cake is set, slice into squares and serve.

BANANA NUTELLA POPSICLES

Popsicles are a great reminder of one's childhood and whenever I lay my eyes on one of these I simply cannot resist. This is one of the easiest recipes to put over-ripe bananas to use.

Servings: 3

Preparation Time: 5 minutes

INGREDIENTS:

- Ripe bananas, 2
- Raw hazelnuts, ¾ cup
- Cocoa powder, 2 tablespoon

METHOD:

1. Process hazelnuts in a blender and form a powdered consistency.
2. Add bananas and cocoa powder and process until combined.
3. Transfer the mixture in Popsicle molds. Push the mixture slightly so that it reaches the surface.
4. Refrigerate the molds for 6 hours.
5. Drizzle chocolate syrup before serving if you like.

Oreo Chocolate Parfait

This is another beautiful treat that will make your guests think you have slaved in the kitchen all day but in reality all you did was mix a few ingredients and blend them. The layers of Oreos are your choice completely. You can make as many layers as you want.

Servings: 4

Preparation Time: 20 minutes

INGREDIENTS:

- Avocados, 2 large, pitted and flesh scooped out
- Coconut oil, 3 teaspoon, melted
- Salt, 1 small pinch
- Maple syrup, ½ cup
- Balsamic, ½ teaspoon
- Vegan dark chocolate, 4 oz.
- Oreos, 10
- Tamari, ½ teaspoon (gluten-free)

METHOD:

1. Melt chocolate and transfer in the blender. Add all the ingredients in the blender except for Oreo's and process for a few minutes until smooth.
2. Crush Oreos and start layering.
3. Prepare individual serving bowls.
4. Spread the layer of Oreos first then top it with chocolate mousse. Spread another layer of Oreos and again spread mousse.
5. Refrigerate for 2 hours before serving.

CONCLUSION

Did you know gluten is one of the hidden reasons behind depression and fatigue? No one enjoys feeling lethargic or depressed. Normally we seek the solution in a cup of coffee or anti-depressants. How many times have we actually thought that the reason could be nothing else but simply our diet? Well, next time try cutting out gluten from your diet and see the results.

Every dessert, mainly cakes; parfait and trifles is made with gluten. Your body finds it hard to break gluten particles and therefore it works 10 times more than it should which as a result affects your health negatively.

Our gluten-free dessert cookbook will teach you 30 simple and delectable dessert recipes with no traces of gluten at all. Some of these recipes use cake/brownie mix bought from the store. Make sure you get yourself the type that clearly states it's gluten-free otherwise all your efforts will be futile.

These gluten-free dessert recipes are very easy, although they require a long freezing time but that shouldn't be a problem. The simple solution to this is to prepare your dessert overnight. This way you will give it plenty of freezing time.

This gluten-free cookbook also features some recipes that are simply made with fruits. So if you are craving something sweet at odd hours just toss the fruits with some sugar, ice cream and whipped cream and your snack is ready.

Try cutting off gluten completely from your diet and observe the enhanced energy levels that you will experience shortly. While going gluten-free you do not have to cut down on a particular meal. You simply have to substitute the ingredients and enjoy your meals in a regular way.

Made in the USA
San Bernardino, CA
15 April 2017